sistakeeper
I define ME!

PLEDGE
READ A-LOUD FOR GIRLS

Tracie Berry-McGhee M.Ed.,LPC

Letter to my SistaKeepers

To all my SistaKeepers please know that this pledge was written just for you to honor yourself as an individual, always remember society does not define you! As you repeat the lines say it with expression, have fun with it, create your own beat! Shout it outloud!
"I define Me!"
End with the SistaKeeper Song!

Nurturing Inner Awareness...
Knowing...

A SistaKeeper is You!

A SistaKeeper is Me!

A SistaKeeper is WE!

sustakeeper

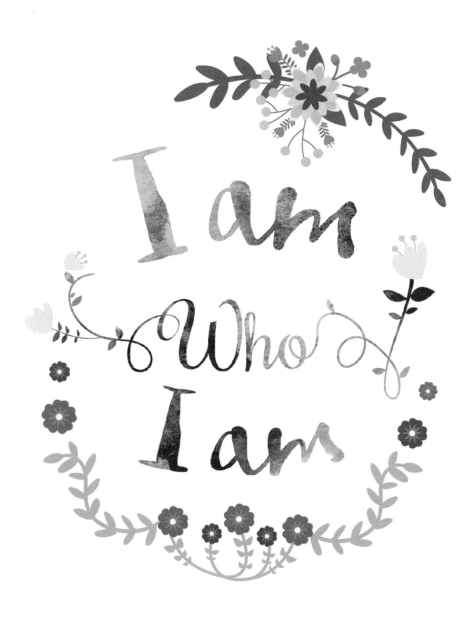

I am
Who
I am

i define me

sistakeeper

I am We

sistakeeper

I am
Diversity

sistakeeper

A mosaic of people live in me

i define me

sistakeeper

sistakeeper

sistakeeper

My story
is my
Legacy

My voice
delivers
Solutions

sistakeeper

My mind seeks Knowledge

sistakeeper

My spirit Flows with purpose

i define me

sistakeeper

I am INSPIRED!

sistakeeper

I am "Empowered"

sistakeeper

I am
Naturally
me

sistakeeper

I hold
The Key
to my destiny

sistakeeper

I DEFINE ME!

sistakeeper

I dedicate this Pledge to all girls!

Define you…

D - Dream Big
E - Educate yourself
F - Faith within
I - Individuality
N - Nia (Purpose)
E - Empower

Designed by Donnie Graphics

sistakeeper

Tracie-Berry McGhee, M.Ed., LPC

Tracie Berry-McGhee, M. Ed., is a native of St. Louis, Mo. A License professional counselor, poet, motivational speaker and founder of a nonprofit organization (501)c3 SistaKeeper Empowerment Center that builds self-awareness, character, diversity and leadership skills in girls. She focuses on nurturing inner awareness in women and girls finding their purpose

As an African-American therapist her mission is to inspire, empower and motivate women and girls to be leaders making a difference in their local, national and global communities. Being a keeper to themselves, bringing awareness to issues that plaque our communities.

www.niagroupstl.com

SistakeeperSTL   ImaKeeper!   Sistakeeper

Made in the USA
Monee, IL
17 July 2023

38987625R00017